The Science of
Ant Communication

Pamela Paterson

৵৵

ISBN: 978-1479174416

Cover by NATWORK, www.natwork.ca

Design by Rhys Griffiths

Edited by Robert Long

Contents

Contents

Preface

Reviewer's Comments

"Nothing is more rewarding than for a teacher to see one of his students take what she learned, enhance it, and present it in a creative and readable way. That is what Pamela has done in this beautiful essay on ant pheromones. It is well worth reading as an example of the complexity of the animal world and the interdependence of behavior and chemistry, the world of chemical ecology." — **Dr. Paul Mazzocchi, Professor Emeritus (Chemistry), University of Maryland.**

Acknowledgements

This book came to be because I am supported by some very fine people. Dr. Paul Mazzocchi, with your extensive knowledge and dedication to the field, impressed upon me the need for quality science as well as competent teachers. Robert Long, with your very generous heart, gave me support for my dreams. And to Kenneth (Congo Man) Kemp, who has more faith and strength than anybody I know, I will always remember I am here today because of you.

The Science of Ant Communication (General Interest Version)

Introduction

Unlike ants themselves, ant communication is no small matter. These tiny creatures have a very sophisticated communication system, and communication drives every facet of their society much like it drives every part of our society.

We use communication to meet our basic needs of finding food. We also use communication to find a mate, raise our children, keep our families safe from threats, establish and defend our territories (even if it's just building a fence to keep the neighbor's dog out), and assess somebody's social status. Throughout history some people have used communication to enslave other people. Ants use communication for the same reasons, even stealing larvae from other colonies and raising these foreign ants as slaves. Ants are more like us than one would think.

Ants have surprisingly creative methods to communicate with each other, and these depend on the species and the message to be communicated. With over 12,000 ant species (1), this makes for a lot of variation for communication.

This book provides an overview of the many forms of ant communication. These tiny creatures are indeed fascinating in how they use communication to spur their fellow members to action in tasks that help the entire colony survive. Not only do ants reflect in many ways who we are, they serve as a good model for us to think about ourselves.

Ants Are Social But Don't Party

Ants are social insects but this does not mean they like to talk to each other at parties. Rather, it means they live in colonies (many generations together) and share tasks that need to be done, whether that is finding food or defending the colony. These colonies or nests may have millions (2) of nestmates. In fact, ants are so well integrated with each other they are sometimes called super organisms because it seems like they operate as a single organism, as one living being instead of individuals.

Communication Through Chemicals

Ants communicate primarily through making and releasing chemicals called pheromones. Using pheromones to communicate is the oldest and most prevalent form of communication among animals (3). Releasing them into the environment influences the behavior in other individuals.

Pheromones are made and released from different glands throughout their body, as shown in part in Figure 1-1. Generally speaking, these glands are located in the three main body sections (head, thorax, and gaster) as well as the legs. Pheromones are released from a number of locations, such as through the mandible (which is the lower jaw in humans) and gaster (which is the end segment furthest from the head). Pheromones are also released from the cuticle, which is the hard, outer layer of their body (4,5,6).

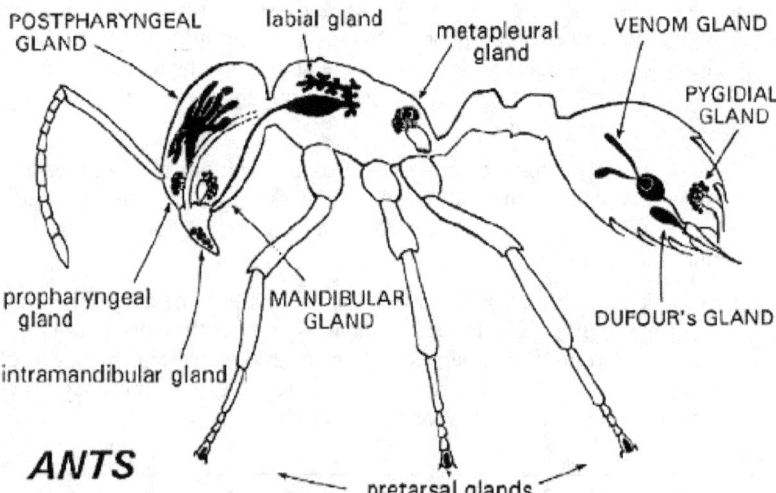

Figure 3-1: Main ant exocrine glands (glands involved in pheromonal functions are in capital letters (7))

To detect pheromones, ants use their antennae. The antennae provide information about where the pheromone is and how strong it is. Given that most ants either have poor eyesight or none (except ones like Australia's bulldog ant, which has excellent vision (8)), detecting pheromones through their antennae provide them with their main source of information. Through antennae, they can, for example, follow trails that lead to food or mark a home territory.

Pheromones for Finding Food

Most people associate ants with picnics, invading the good mood and moving in on the food. Animations would have you believe they can carry away an entire pie by themselves, throwing it on their backs and marching it down the trail. While it is true that ants engage in food–finding expeditions, how they do this is far from just throwing a pie on their backs.

To begin with, a scout is sent out from the colony to find food. (As a side note, ants are even clever about who they choose for this dangerous mission, some preferring to select their most expendable members just in case they do not return.) After the scout finds food, the scout lays down a trail pheromone to create the trail. The better the food source, the stronger trail they create (9).

Next, other foragers (ants that find food) come to help move the food. When they arrive, they also lay down more pheromones, thus reinforcing the trail (10). If there is a substantial amount of food, coworkers who return to the nest are "smelled" by others, who in turn join the effort to help move the food (11). These ants are surrounded by helpful coworkers, for should one of them get lost on the way to the food, another ant will touch its antennae to guide it back onto the trail (12).

Ants may follow trails created only by their own species. They may also be less particular and follow trails by other species (13). Regardless of whose trail it is, using pheromones to find food has enabled ants to find and feast on those big picnics.

Phenomenal Pheromones—Know Their Strength

Remember how strong that perfume was in the elevator? It affected everybody just by diffusing through the air. While some people's perfume may last only a few hours, others might last for days. Pheromones work the same way.

Some pheromones vaporize after a few minutes while others can last for several days—because they need to. In the case of the Malaysian ponerine army ant, its pheromone to attract ants to come quickly and kill the prey lasts only five minutes. There is no need to keep attracting ants for hours to help in this fast–moving maneuver. However, another pheromone which tells workers how to find their way back to the colony lasts longer at 25 minutes, which is enough time for them to make the journey home (14).

Like the Malaysian ponerine, the Pharaoh's ant also has pheromones for prey kills and trail–finding, but its long–term trail pheromone can last for several days not 25 minutes. It also has a pheromone which serves to chemically block the branches on the trail that are not used so ants do not get lost, like a "do not enter" sign (15).

Unique Blends of Pheromones Just Like Coffee

Not only do pheromones have different strengths, they also can be made of one or more compounds in a blend like coffee. These blends allow for more precise communication because the signal would be very specific to its own species. Different species have their own unique blends, just like those coffee commercials. For example, in the leafcutter ant, its trail pheromone is made of two compounds in a blend of 14 parts to 1 part (16).

In addition, compounds may be used in a specific order. Such is the case with the army ant. To incite other ants to follow the trail, one compound is released to the workers, followed by a second compound (17). Or, ants may opt for releasing multiple compounds from several glands—this is what the African weaver ant does in its alarm response and defense system (18).

The notion that coffee connoisseurs have their own blends unique to their own tastes, and the most elite of them consider themselves to be in a separate class in this regard is also found in pheromones. The actual blend of compounds differs among species, and ant species will respond differently even to the same pheromone (19). Even ants within the same colony respond differently, depending on their caste (level in their society) (20). Ants of different castes may not even have the same pheromones—for example, in the weaver ant (*Oecophylla longinoda*) the primary workers have the alarm stimuli (21).

Pheromones for Fighting

When there is an immediate threat to an ant or the colony—for example, when an ant is crushed, a predator is in the vicinity, or the nest caves in— ants release alarm pheromones. These pheromones can make ants aggressive and incite them to attack or cause them to go into "panic" mode, and they retreat or hide (22).

Ants use pheromones to mark their territories, as other animals do, to advertise their territory and deter invasions. Ants that live in the same nest can recognize these pheromones and are safe, but ants from other nests are not welcome. Should an ant from a different colony try to deposit pheromones there, the ants may become aggressive and quickly recruit an army to deal with the invader. Ants don't fool around when it comes to their territory (23).Well, neither do humans. Have you ever tried jumping over the neighbor's fence as a shortcut to the convenience store?

It has been said that people living in the same house are like family, regardless of whether they actually are. The same notion can be applied in the ant world. If an ant is living in the colony, even if it is not closely related to the others, it is treated like family. On the other hand, ants of the same species but living in different nests may be treated aggressively because they have a different odor (every colony has its own odor) (24). Does this mean that ants who smell together, stay together?

Hydrocarbons Are for Communicating, Not Just Crude Oil

In addition to pheromones, a second way ants communicate is through touching another ant's cuticle, which is the hard outer layer. The cuticle contains chemicals called hydrocarbons, which consists only of hydrogen and carbon in varying amounts. Hydrocarbons occur naturally in the earth such as in crude oil. Hydrocarbons in the ant cuticle are known to prevent the ant from losing moisture, and contain a wealth of information (25).

Cuticular hydrocarbons provide information about sex, age, colony, and reproductive status. Each hydrocarbon has a different odor that provides ants different signals, such as their tasks (for example, foraging) or whether they are from the same colony. Hydrocarbons can also be sex attractants or be used for recognizing nestmates (26). These hydrocarbons also seem to allow ants to recognize fertile and infertile nestmates (27).

There is a tremendous amount of variation in hydrocarbon types, depending on the task needed to be done (28, 29). In the red harvester ant, ants involved in nest maintenance have different hydrocarbon types than foragers in the outside environment (30).

Interestingly, foragers will not leave the nest to find food if the scouts searching for food each morning do not return safely. In fact, in order for foragers to leave the nest, hydrocarbons need to be placed near the nest entrance in the right order at the correct time of the day (when the colony is ready to begin foraging).

This was revealed when scientists removed patrollers and replaced them with beads that were scented with varying levels of hydrocarbons. The foragers touched the beads with their antennae, and would only begin foraging if they detected the same concentrations of hydrocarbons as released by the scouts, and at the correct time of the day (31). Now, that's picky.

Let's Communicate by Making Noise or Dance Moves

A third way ants communicate is physically, either by touching each other or rubbing parts of their body with another part to make sound. When children do this to make odd sounds, it makes them laugh, but for ants it can signal many messages, including "somebody found food" and "I'm in danger." They make sound vibrations by using a scraper on the top of their body to rub against ridges located near the end of the body on the gaster (32). The sound travels along the ground or perhaps in the air and other ants receive the signal (33).

One example of this vibrational communication is found among ants that live in tree nests made from larval silk. If the nest is disturbed, they produce an alarm response: they drum their abdomens on the nest. Other ants follow suit, and in time the entire nest is aware of the threat. This sound is louder than humans talking (34). How would this work for humans, drumming their bellies on the floor of their homes to raise the alarm?

Carpenter ants also use vibrational communication by drumming with mandibles and gasters to transmit a signal. Fellow nestmates respond by aggressively defending the nest and removing dependent nestmates (35).

These vibration signals are also used if leafcutter ants are in distress themselves. For example, if they are buried alive from the nest caving in, they send vibration signals to their nestmates, who then rescue them (36).

In addition, when leafcutter ant workers make sound, they are telling others they have found a valuable leaf. The vibrations travel along the leaf–cutting ant's body and into the ground through the ant's head. Not only do the vibrations help with the actual leaf cutting, they also help recruit other ants (37).

Another ant species, upon finding food that is too large to move by itself, releases poison into the air. When help arrives from its nestmates, these newcomers in turn release more poison into the air and also make sound, causing even more ants to come. Releasing both poison into the air and making sound results in more assistance than by releasing poison alone (38).

While people do not vibrate to communicate with each other, both humans and ants use physical gestures. Ants have a repertoire of "dance moves" they can use. In weaver ants, they release pheromones from the rectal gland to recruit other ants for food expeditions and defending territories, and then use physical movements to communicate their messages. For food recruitment, they wave their heads in a lateral direction at the same time they open their mandibles. For defending territories, they use jerking movements that resemble those of an actual attack (39).

Let's Communicate by Running Together

When you think of tandem bicycles, maybe an image comes to mind of two people on a two–seated bicycle with a common goal of getting to a destination. Now think about "tandem running."

"Tandem running" or "tandem calling" is a fascinating type of communication between two ants in which one ant is the leader and the other ant is the student. The leader and student run together to the food, continually adjusting the speed and direction as they go as per their communication signals (40).

In the European ant (*Temnothorax albipennis*), the leader only continues to show the student where the food is if the follower's antennae continually tap the leader on the legs and abdomen (in the end gaster section). The distance between leader and follower, from the point of the leader's gaster to the follower's head, is an average of an astounding one millimeter (41).

And, when the leader and follower get too close, the leader speeds up and the follower slows down in order to restore the one millimeter distance. If the leader and the follower are too far apart (the distance of twice the length of the follower's antennae), the leader stops and waits for the follower (42). Now, how nice is that!

As a side note, the antennae position is integral to the success of the tandem run, for when *Temnothorax albipennis* were carried to the food source—in a backwards and inverted position—they could not teach other ants where the food source was (43).

It is interesting to note that the leader, by itself, could do the run at four times the speed than when it is engaged in a tandem run. Having a follower slows the leader down because the follower loops in circles, looking for landmarks. So why do ants engage in tandem running if it is slower for the leader? Because it decreases the time needed for the follower to find food, for example, from 310 seconds to an average of 201 seconds. (The follower, in six out of eight instances, actually takes its own route back to the colony which is a more linear route.) Tandem running also appears to be a way to enhance the collective knowledge of the colony, for tandem followers become tandem leaders and show others where the food is (44).

Tandem running can also be used for purposes other than finding food. Should *Leptothorax albipennis* require a new nest due to damage, they use tandem running to show other nestmates the potential colony location. After a number of nestmates learn of the new location, they change from tandem running to carrying the remaining nestmates (45).

While tandem running is a fascinating mode of ant communication, it is actually an older form of communication developed before odor–trail communication and sex attraction. Tandem running is not as advanced as trail pheromones, and is used in small food finds (46).

What Do Brains and Queens Have to Do With It?

What do brains and queens have to do with ant communication? Complex behaviors are related to, in part, brain size (more neurons) and environmental factors. In ants, a bigger brain is closely linked with a bigger antennal lobe, which is the part of the brain that is involved in processing olfactory (that is, "smelling") information. Presumably, with a larger antennal lobe the ant has a greater ability to process olfactory information (47).

In addition to the brain size, whether the queen is present also appears to be a guiding force in how ants behave. In carpenter ants, when the queen was present workers attacked kin and non–kin at an equal rate. However, when workers were raised away from the colony, they were essentially tolerant of each other but just more aggressive toward non–kin. Diet was also noted as a factor in the level of aggression (48).

Ants Do Not Communicate Directly

In understanding the dynamics of ant communication, it is important to note that communication signals do not elicit specific and direct behavioral responses. This means that ants do not consciously send out a message such as "go and find food" and another ant acts on it: "well, it's cold out there but all right, we're hungry."

Rather, communication among ants is much more subtle than that. Ants will send out certain communication signals which *increase the probability* that other ants will change their behavior a certain way in response to the stimuli. In basic terms, it could be thought of like this: "If Bill ate all his roommate's food, this increases the probability that his roommate will buy more food." Of course, it doesn't guarantee that's what his roommate will do (especially if Bill makes a habit of eating his food), but it is likely to be at least one of the results.

This is called modulatory communication: "Modulatory signals are devices for shifting the threshold for the releasing effectiveness of other stimuli, thus enhancing the behavioral response to them." (49)

Conclusion

This discussion of ant communication has shown that their communication is an impressive and complex interaction between members and their society. Ants communicate through pheromone chemicals, touching each other, and making sounds. Unlike their physical stature, ant communication is indeed no small matter.

The Science of Ant Communication (Scientific Version)

Introduction

Unlike ants themselves, ant communication is no small matter. Ants have an extensive communication system and communicate with each other on every level of their society—to find food, mate, raise their young, identify and exclude foreigners, establish and defend territories, determine caste, and steal larvae from other colonies to raise as slaves.

These tiny creatures are regulated by the "precise transmission of social signals in time and space" (50) through a few modalities: pheromones (compounds that elicit specific responses in conspecifics), cuticular hydrocarbons, and physical (tactile or through sound). These modalities may be used singularly or in combination with each other, as the ways in which ants communicate are as varied as the message being communicated and the species themselves.

This book provides an overview of the many forms of ant communication, and presents information about ant physiology as it relates to communication, communication theory, and the various modalities pertaining to how they are used by several species.

Ant Physiology

To understand ant communication, some basic physiology must be known. While many parts of ants are involved in communication, the main body parts of ants that are involved in communication are the two antennae (attached to the head), many glands (refer to Figure 2-1), waxy cuticular exterior, and stridulation mechanism.

Ant antennae are olfactory (smelling) organs that allow them to sense other ant pheromones. The antennae provide information about the direction as well as intensity (that is, strength) of the pheromones. As the eyesight is either poor or non–existent (except ones like Australia's bulldog ant, which has excellent vision (51)) it is the antennae that provide the main mechanism for receiving stimuli. Each antenna is comprised of two major parts: a long scape attached to the head and about 10 segments together called the funiculus (52).

Ants also have exocrine glands located throughout their bodies, as shown in part in Figure 2-1. Note that this figure is intended to show the main gland areas for illustrative purposes. Additional glands have been found in some species, such as the epithelial gland in the tibia of the front and hind legs, and three secretory cells in the hind leg tibia in the ponerine ants (53). Some of these glands (in capital letters) synthesize pheromones, which are then released from the ant in a number of ways, such as through the mandibles (54) or gaster, which is the equivalent of an ant abdomen. A gaster has five segments, and a terminal stinger (or pore) that acid can be sprayed through.

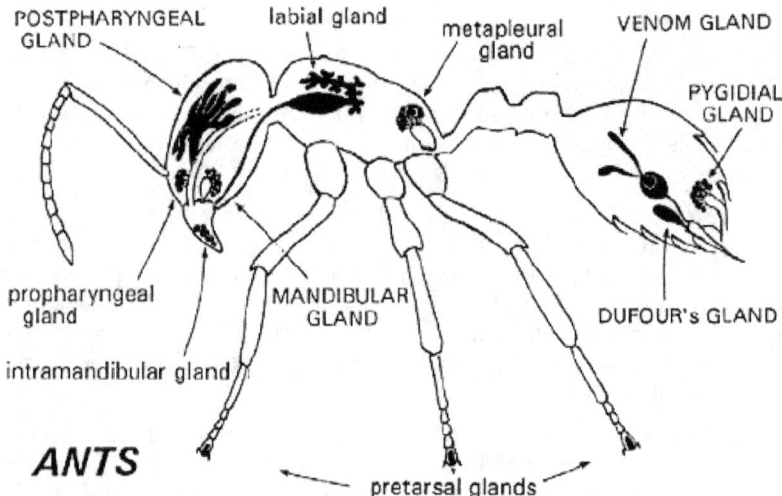

POSTPHARYNGEAL GLAND

labial gland

metapleural gland

VENOM GLAND

PYGIDIAL GLAND

propharyngeal gland

MANDIBULAR GLAND

DUFOUR's GLAND

intramandibular gland

ANTS

pretarsal glands

Figure 4-1: Main ant exocrine glands (glands involved in pheromonal functions are in capital letters) (55)

Pheromones are not only found in glands. They are also found in the ant epicuticular waxy surface. Hydrocarbons in the ant cuticle are known to prevent the ant from losing moisture; they also have a function in ant communication by assisting them to identify their nestmates (56).

The last part of ant physiology involved in communication is for physical communication, through direct touch or sound vibrations produced by their stridulation mechanism. Stridulation occurs when ants use a scraper (which is located at the posterior dorsal margin of the postpetiole) against parallel ridges on the anterior of the ant (located at the first gastral tergite) (57).

About Ant Communication

Ants are social insects that are organized in colonies, nests, or super colonies that may contain millions (58) of nestmates. Ant colonies are sometimes called super organisms because they operate like a single organism in the way that they seamlessly communicate with each other. Ants in a colony have specific roles and carry out tasks according to their role. There are, for example, workers, harvesters, foragers, scouts, and defenders. In understanding the context of ant communication, it should be noted that communication signals among ants do not elicit specific and direct behavioral responses. Rather, there is a link between the signals transmitted and the behavioral response:

"Communication in complex social systems is not always characterized by a deterministic releasing process but sometimes plays a more subtle role. For example, in a group of ant workers certain communication signals suffice to adjust the behavior of group mates towards one another. These signals have the effect of shifting the probability for the performance of other behavioral acts, but they do not elicit particular behavioral responses. We have called this kind of communication system 'modulatory communication'. Modulatory signals are devices for shifting the threshold for releasing effectiveness of other stimuli, thus enhancing the behavioral response to them." (59)

Multimodal Communication

Ants engage in multimodal communication to enhance the effectiveness of the communication. Modality refers to the mode of communication, such as through pheromones, cuticular hydrocarbons, or physical (that is, tactile or sound vibrations).

So, ants release pheromones from their glands and cuticle. Ants also send sound vibrations through their stridulation mechanism, and other ants receive signals from stridulation through the substrate. It is speculated that ants may also receive these signals through the air (60).

Ants also use physical communication in a number of ways. For example, weaver ants (*Oecophylla*), in addition to releasing pheromones from the rectal gland for food and territorial defense recruitment, use jerking movements that resemble those of an actual attack and, in food recruitment, wave their heads in a lateral direction at the same time they open their mandibles (61).

In ants, one signal can modulate another that is of a different modality. For example, a forager of the species *A. cockerelli* or *A. albisetosus*, upon finding food too large to be carried or dragged by itself, releases poison gland secretions into the air. Ants from the same nest travel to help move the food, even if it is two meters away. When they arrive, these ants release the poison gland pheromone and stridulate, in turn attracting more ants to the food source faster than if they had only released the pheromone. The food is removed to the nest one to two minutes earlier because multiple modalities are used (62).

In the leafcutter ant (*Atta cephalotes*), the workers stridulate when cutting a valuable leaf. The stridulatory vibrations travel along the leaf–cutting ant's body and into the substrate through the ant's head. Not only do the vibrations help with the cutting process, they also enhance the chemical recruitment signal that was laid through poison gland secretions. Although the original purpose of the vibrations may have been to help with the cutting, they evolved into a modulatory signal and then a signal for recruiting. In another study, the stridulatory vibrations were shown to function as stress and rescue signals (63).

Pheromones

Communication through chemical signaling using pheromones is the oldest and most prevalent form of communication among animals (64). Pheromones can be used as odor trails, and differ from species to species regarding where they are synthesized in the body, what their chemical composition is, and how long they last. Most of the pheromones in ants contain between 5 and 20 carbon atoms; the molecular weight of each is between 80 and 300 (65).

Pheromones may be released to the substrate or embedded in food that is given from one ant to another (known as trophallaxis). The pheromones are detected in the receiver's antennae. Note that the level of volatility of the pheromones differs among species. For example, in fire ants, the trail chemical from the Dufour's gland is laid down by the stinger and these molecules evaporate very quickly. On the other hand, in some carpenter ants, the trail pheromones (which are synthesized in the hind gut), will last many days (66).

There may be 105 different exocrine glands among social insects (not just ants) that release pheromones (67). In *Leptogenys* species *Megaponera foetens*, a predatory raider, one recruitment component is secreted from the poison gland but a second recruitment pheromone, (3R,4S)-4-methyl-3-heptanol, is secreted from the pygidial gland. The poison gland secretions are used more for orientation while the secretions in the pygidial gland are for recruitment (68). In the genus *Onychomyrmex*, trail pheromones for group raiding and colony emigration are from the sternal gland; the orientation pheromone is from a basitarsal gland in the hind legs (69).

Pheromones exist for a general or species–specific purpose. In the genus *Myrmica*, the ants produce recruitment signals (for foraging) in the poison gland that are not species–specific, and also produce species–specific hydrocarbon mixtures in the Dufour's glands that mark the home area. It has been suggested that there is no need for the recruitment signals to be species–specific as they are very volatile, but the species–specific Dufour's gland secretions likely mark trunk routes which also have colony–specific markers (70).

Compounds and Concentrations

Pheromones can consist of one substance for a specific function or multiple components, possibly in a specific blend. Two examples of the "single compound concept" include methyl 4-methylpyrrole-2-carboxylate, from the *Atta texana's* venom gland, and faranal from the *Monomorium pharaonis's* gland (71). Multi–component pheromones, where the pheromone is a mixture of one or more substances, provides for a higher specificity in signaling among the same species, particularly when many species use the same substance.

For example, in *Tetramorium caespitum* the trail pheromone is a 70:30 ratio of 2,5-dimethylpyrazine and 3-ethyl-2,5-dimethylpyrazine from the venom gland. This ratio has been proven to be the most effective in terms of ants following it. In another example, the leaf–cutting ant (*Atta sexdens*) has, for the best trail–following behavior, a 14:1 mixture of 3-ethyl-2,5-dimethylpyrazine and 4-methylpyrrole-2-carboxylate, as found in its venom gland. In ponerine ant (*Leptogenys peuqueti*), 14 compounds were identified in the trail pheromone (72). At times, the multiple substances work in conjunction with each other. The army ant (*Aenictus* sp.) requires two substances in its postpygidial gland to incite trail–following behavior: methyl anthranilate and methyl nicotinate. Methyl anthranilate, at 1% of the secretion, has a primer effect and makes the workers sensitive to methyl nicotinate (73).

Not only may there be multiple compounds from one gland in a pheromone response, there may be multiple glands involved. For example, in *Acanthomyops claviger*, both the mandibular gland and the Dufour's gland are involved in an alarm response. In the African weaver ant *Oecophylla longinoda*, the mandibular, venom, and Dufour's glands are involved in the alarm/defense system (74).

The glands, in addition to containing pheromones, can contain many other substances. For example, in the carpenter ant *Camponotus ligniperda*, there are least 41 compounds. In the mandibular glands of the weaver ant (*Oecophylla longinoda*), there are over 30 compounds. The compounds are found in different levels for various colonies (75). In the case of many of the Myrmicine ant species, these substances are involved in the biosynthetic pathway: trail pheromones (which contain nitrogen, such as in pyrazines or pyrroles) are actually byproducts of the pathways in which venom is synthesized. Both the venom and the pheromone are released through the stinger (76).

Cuticular Hydrocarbons

Cuticular hydrocarbons have been analyzed to reveal information about sex, age, colony, and reproductive status. Each hydrocarbon has a different odor that provides ants different signals, such as their tasks (for example, foraging) or whether they are from the same colony. These long–chained cuticular hydrocarbons can also be sex attractants or be used for recognizing nestmates. They are altered at the onset or decline of the time of egg–laying: in the queen, oenocytes (glandular cells in the body) produce cuticular hydrocarbons; these glandular secretions are released in the hemolymph and then transported to the cuticle. Cuticular hydrocarbons also seem to allow ants to recognize fertile and infertile nestmates, although specific cuticular compounds for this purpose have not yet been isolated (77). It is suggested that the postpharyngeal gland may have a role in producing the cuticular hydrocarbons, as similar hydrocarbons found in the cuticle have also been found in the postpharyngeal gland (78).

As cuticular hydrocarbons are not volatile, they can only be perceived through direct contact through, for example, the antennae. It was found among *M. Gulosa* that workers needed direct contact to determine that the queen was present. In larger colonies, where workers may not have direct contact with the queen, the queen pheromones are transmitted other ways, such as through other workers or the substrate (79).

In the red harvester ant (*Pogonomyrmex barbatus*), the cuticular hydrocarbon profile varies among tasks. Foragers in the outside environment (where it is warmer and drier) have higher ratios of n-alkanes than ants involved in nest maintenance. If red harvester scouts canvassing the area around the colony for food each morning do not return safely, the foragers will not leave the nest. It is not just the presence of hydrocarbons that spur the forager ants into action—the hydrocarbons need to be deposited near the nest entrance in the proper sequence at the correct time of the day (when the colony is ready to begin foraging). This was revealed when scientists removed patrollers and replaced them with beads that were scented with varying levels of hydrocarbons. The foragers touched the beads with their antennae, and would only begin foraging if they detected the same concentrations of hydrocarbons as in the scouts at the correct time of the day (80).

Tactile Communication

There are a number of ways in which ants employ tactile communication, either through direct contact or substrate–borne vibrations, separately or in conjunction with other communication modalities. Examples of tactile communication include grooming nestmates, alarming nestmates to potential threats, and showing where a food source is through waggling and jerking. Ants are also known to touch each other's antennae when they pass each other on the trail, although the reason for this has not been determined (81). As sound is faster than pheromone molecules traveling through air (and ants have no ears), substrate–borne vibration communication is effectively used in situations that require urgency. However, it has also been noted that sound is distorted through the substrate, in particular over distance (82).

Camponotus senex ants live in arboreal nests (up to one meter in length) made from larval silk. If the nest is disturbed by physical means or by carbon dioxide, they produce an alarm response: they drum their abdomens on the nest substrate. Other ants follow suit, and in time the entire nest is aware of the threat. This sound is also detectable by human ears—it is louder than humans talking (83). Carpenter ants (genus *Camponotus*) drum with mandibles and gasters to transmit a vibration signal. Fellow nestmates respond by aggressively defending the nest and removing dependent nestmates. If leafcutter ants are buried alive from the nest caving in, they are rescued by alerting their nestmates through substrate vibration (84).

To recruit other nestmates to a food site, *Aphaenogaster albisetosus* rub their abdominal tergites together to make sound (that is, stridulate), in addition to releasing the recruitment pheromone from the poison gland. In response to the stridulation, other workers release additional pheromone, thus facilitating faster recruitment to the food site than with pheromone alone (85).

Specific Ant Behaviors

Many ant behaviors in relation to communication have already been discussed. Now, a few of those behaviors as well as others, such as foraging, tandem running, responding to alarms, and establishing and defending territories will be explored in greater detail.

Foraging

The familiar comic scene of the ants carrying away the picnic food is an example of cooperation among ants. The scout who finds the food creates the initial trail by laying down a trail pheromone. (The better the food source, the stronger trail they create. (86)) The trail is then reinforced by other foragers, as they come to assist in transporting the food (87). If there is a substantial source of food, after coworkers have returned to the nest with some food, other ants smell their body odor and travel to the food source. If an ant loses its way from the trail, it will travel in circles until it finds the trail, or another worker will direct the lost ant by touching its antennae (88).

Some species respond only to their own trails, while others respond to their own trails as well as the trails of other species. For example, in two species of *Aphaenogaster* that are closely related, *A. cockerelli* follows only its own trail but *A. albisetosus* follows its trail as well as the trail of *A. cockerelli*. The main recruitment pheromone of *A. cockerelli* is (R)-(+)-1-phenylethanol and the main recruitment pheromone of *A. albisetosus* is 4-methyl-3-heptanone. *A. cockerelli* also contains 4-methyl-3-heptanone and 4-methyl-3-heptanol, but the workers do not respond to these secretions. *A. albisetosus* responds to 4-methyl-3-heptanone in the *A. cockerelli* secretions but not the phenylethanol (89).

The Malaysian ponerine army ant (*Leptogenys distinguenda*) trail pheromones from the poison gland and the pygidial gland have different functions. The poison gland has two pheromone components—one is for attracting to prey items on a powerful, short–term basis (very volatile and only lasts five minutes), while the other directs workers back to the colony as they may have become disoriented after the attacking frenzy (produced in the pygidial gland, it lasts 25 minutes). The pre–attraction component is strong so that the ants come quickly and can defeat the prey, but they do not stay attracted past the amount of time that help is needed. After the prey has succumbed, they do not need as strong of a pheromone to go back to the colony. A few ants could leave a powerful enough trail to attract many nestmates (90).

Like the Malaysian ponerine army ant, the Pharaoh's ant (*Monomorium pharaonis*) has short–term (for pre–attraction) and long–term (for finding the trail between the colony and the prey) trail pheromones. Its long–term trail pheromone can last for several days. It also has a short–term repellent pheromone, which serves to chemically block the branches on the trail that are not used so ants do not get lost. Likely they use additional pheromones along with multiple modalities of communication to increase the catalog of messages (91).

Tandem Running

"Tandem running" or "tandem calling" is a fascinating example of communication between two ants in which one ant is the leader and the other ant is the student. It is an elaborate and complex process in which velocity and direction in the run are continually adjusted according to the constant communication signals between each other as they run to the food. Tandem running is the evolutionary precursor of odor–trail communication and sex attraction. Note that it is not as advanced as pheromone trails and is only used in small food finds (92).

In *Temnothorax albipennis*, the leader only continues to show the student where the food is if the follower's antennae continually tap the leader on the legs and abdomen (in the gaster section). The distance between leader and follower, from the point of the leader's gaster to the follower's head, is an average of an astounding one millimeter. When the leader and follower get too close, the leader speeds up and the follower slows down in order to restore the one millimeter distance. If the leader and the follower are too far apart (the distance of twice the length of the follower's antennae), the leader stops and waits for the follower. As a side note, the antennae position is integral to the success of the tandem run, for when *Temnothorax albipennis* were carried to the food source—in a backwards and inverted position—they could not teach other ants where the food source was (93).

It is interesting to note that the leader, by itself, could do the run at four times the speed than when it is engaged in a tandem run. Having a follower slows the leader down because the follower loops in circles, looking for landmarks. So why do ants engage in tandem running if it is slower for the leader? Because it decreases the time needed for the follower to find food, from 310 seconds to a mean of 201 seconds. (The follower, in six out of eight instances, actually takes its own route back to the colony which is a more linear route.) Tandem running also appears to be a way to enhance the collective knowledge of the colony, for tandem followers become tandem leaders and show others where the food is (94).

Responding to Alarms

Alarm pheromones are released when there is an immediate threat to an ant or the colony, such as when an ant is crushed, a predator is in the vicinity, or the nest caves in. Some alarm pheromones make ants aggressive and incite them to attack while other alarm pheromones incite ants into "panic" mode, and they retreat or hide (95).

Just as in the other types of ant chemicals, there is no "one size fits all" when it comes to alarm pheromones. For example, while many species of the family Formicinae have undecane in the Dufour's glands, other hydrocarbons are also involved, and the total blend of these substances is species–specific (96). Different species of ants respond differently, even to the same pheromone (97). Furthermore, even within the same colony various castes identify with a specific blend of the same alarm pheromone. The various castes of the leafcutter *Atta* respond to different blends of the same alarm pheromone components (98). In the African weaver ant (*Oecophylla longinoda*) the primary and other workers have different chemical compositions of the mandibular gland secretion, and only the primary workers have the alarm stimuli (99).

Establishing and Defending Territories

Ants establish and defend their territories in a number of ways through pheromones and tandem running.

Even ants of the same species—but from different nests—may be treated aggressively because a specific colony has its own odor. Ants of the same colony are usually more closely related, but not always. However, they are treated like family regardless of whether they actually are (100). Primary workers of the African weaver ant (*Oecophylla longinoda*) mark their territories with pheromones, and these pheromones are recognized by their nestmates. If they detect that an ant from a different colony is depositing pheromones, they become aggressive and rapidly recruit nestmates to the area. These ants use pheromones to advertise territories and deter invasions (101). Should *Leptothorax albipennis* require a new nest due to damage, they use tandem running to show other nestmates the potential colony location. After a number of nestmates learn of the new location, they change from tandem running to carrying their remaining nestmates (102).

Conclusion

While ants have developed complex communication systems involving pheromones, cuticular hydrocarbons, and physical touch and sound, these modalities are not the only determinants of behavior in ants. Behavioral complexity is related to, in part, brain size (more neurons) and environmental factors. The size of the antennal lobe is also highly correlated with brain size. Presumably, with a larger antennal lobe the ant has a greater ability to process olfactory information (103).

Ants are also affected by social structure; that is, whether a queen is present. In carpenter ants (*Camponotus* spp.), when workers removed as pupae from the colony were raised away from the colony, they were essentially tolerant of each other but were more aggressive toward non–kin. The aggressiveness was also affected somewhat by diet. Then, when a queen was present, workers attacked both kin and non–kin at an equal rate, independent of diet (104).

This examination of ant communication has shown that it is a complex, multi–faceted interaction between members and their society. While the majority of ant communication involves pheromones, other environmental factors and communication modalities are used to enhance the effectiveness of ant–to–ant communication. Ant communication is indeed no small matter.

Partial List of Pheromones

This appendix contains a partial list of pheromones to illustrate the diverse chemicals used in ant communication (105):

- **Alcohol:** Ethanol, Methyl heptanol
- **Aldehyde:** Hexanal
- **Carboxylic acid:** Formic acid
- **Ester:** Decyl acetate
- **Hydrocarbon (alkane):** Hexane, Undecane
- **Ketone:** Methyl heptanone
- **Terpenoid:** Citronellal

Notes

1   Agosti et al

2   Traniello

3   Traniello

4   Tijskens et al

5   Traniello

6   Yusuf et al

7   Billen

8   Moffett

9   Holldobler

10   Traniello

11   Moody

12   Moody

13   Holldobler

14   Jackson et al

15   Jackson et al

16   Billen

17   Billen

18   Billen

19   Traniello

20   Jackson et al

21   Billen

22   Traniello

23   Holldobler and Wilson

24   Holldobler

25   Yusuf et al

26   Dietemann et al

27   Dietemann et al

28   Dietemann et al

29   Green et al

30   Green et al

31   Green et al

32   Hill

33   Hill

34   Jackson et al

35   Hill

36   Hill

37   Holldobler

38   Holldobler

39   Holldobler

40   Moody

41   Franks and Richardson

42   Franks and Richardson

43   Franks and Richardson

44   Franks and Richardson

45   Pratt et al

46   Moody

47   Cold

48   Holldobler

49   Holldobler

50   Holldobler

51   Moffett

52   Traniello

53   Tijskens et al

54   Traniello

55   Billen

56   Yusuf et al

57   Billen

58   Traniello

59   Holldobler

60   Billen

61   Holldobler

62   Holldobler

63   Holldobler

64   Traniello

65   Billen

66   Klotz

67   Billen

68   Holldobler

69   Holldobler

70   Holldobler

71   Billen

72   Billen

73   Billen

74   Billen

75   Holldobler

76   Billen

77   Dietemann et al

78   Billen

79   Dietemann et al

80   Green et al

81 Jackson et al

82 Virant-Doberlet and Cokl

83 Jackson et al

84 Hill

85 Jackson et al

86 Holldobler

87 Traniello

88 Moody

89 Holldobler

90 Jackson et al

91 Jackson et al

92 Moody

93 Franks and Richardson

94 Franks and Richardson

95 Traniello

96 Holldobler

97 Traniello

98 Jackson et al

99 Billen

100 Holldobler

101 Holldobler and Wilson

102 Pratt et al

103 Cold

104 Holldobler

105 Traniello

References

Agosti, D, and NF Johnson. Editors. 2005. Antbase. World Wide Web electronic publication. antbase.org, version (05/2005).

Billen, Johan. "Signal variety and communication in social insects." Proc. Neth. Entomol. Soc. Meet. Vol. 17, 2006.

Cold, Blaine. "Size and behavior in ants: Constraints on complexity." Proc. Natl. Acad. Sci. Vol. 82, 8548-8551, December 1985.

Dietemann, V, C Peeters, J Liebig, V Thivet, and B Hölldobler. "Myrmecia gulosa the ant Cuticular hydrocarbons mediate discrimination of reproductives and nonreproductives in the ant Myrmecia gulosa." Proceedings of the National Academy of Sciences of the United States of America website. July 2003.

Franks, Nigel R. and Tom Richardson. "Teaching in tandem-running ants." Brief Communications. Nature Publishing Group. 2006.

Green, Michael and Deborah Gordon. "Cuticular hydrocarbons inform task decisions." Nature. Vol. 423, May 1 2003.

Hill, Peggy. "Vibration and Animal Communication: A Review." American Zoology, Vol. 41, 1135-1142, 2001.

Holldobler, Bert. "The Chemistry of Social Regulation: Multicomponent Signals in Ant Societies." Proc. Natl. Acad. Sci. Vol. 92, 19-22, January 1995.

Holldobler, Bert and E.O. Wilson. "(Latreille) Colony-Specific Territorial Pheromone in the African Weaver Ant Oecophylla Longinoda." Proc. Natl. Acad. Sci. Vol. 74, No. 5, 2072-2075, May 1977.

Jackson, Duncan, and Francis L.W. Ratnieks. "Communication in ants." Current Biology Vol. 16, No. 15.

Klotz, J, D Williams, B Reid, K Vail, and P Koehler. "Ant Trails: A Key to Management with Baits." Florida Institute of Food and Agricultural Sciences. 2000.

Moffett, Mark. "Bulldog Ants." National Geographic website. May 2007.

Moody, Dwight. "Chapter 7: A Field Study of the Ant Trail Phenomenon." Tested Studies for Laboratory Teaching. Vol 5, 1993.

Morgan, D, RR Do Nascimento, SJ Keegans, and J Billen. "Comparative Study of Mandibular Gland Secretions of Workers of Ponerine Ants." Journal of Chemical Ecology. Vol. 25, No. 6, 1999.

Pratt, S, EB Mallon, DJT Sumpter, and NR Franks. "Quorum sensing, recruitment, and collective decision-making during colony emigration by the ant *Leptothorax albipennis*." Behav. Ecol. Sociobol., 52:117-127, 2002.

Tijskens, M, F Ito, and J Billen. "Novel Exocrine Glands in the Legs of the Ponerine *Ant Amblyopone Reclinata* (Hymenoptera, Formicidae)." Netherlands Journal of Zoology. Vol. 52, No. 1, 69-75, 2002.

Traniello, James. "Chapter 10: Olfaction and Chemical Communication." Boston University, Department of Biology. 1996.

Virant-Doberlet, M and Andrej Cokl. "Vibrational Communication in Insects." Neotropical Entomology. Vol. 33, No. 2, 121-134, 2004.

Yusuf, AA, CW Pirk, RM Crewe, PG Njagi, I Gordon, and B Torto. "Nestmate recognition and the role of cuticular hydrocarbons in the African termite raiding ant Pachycondyla analis." Journal of Chemical Ecology. Vol. 36, No. 4, 441-8. April 2010.

About the Author

When she is not admiring ants, Pamela Paterson spends her time as a writing consultant, college instructor, and speaker.

Pamela has written hundreds of articles, papers, and books in over 30 subject areas. The topics she writes about ranges from business to science to health, and everything in between.

She has a bachelor's degree in journalism and a master's degree in science from the University of Maryland. Pamela was recently inducted into the same honor society as Jimmy Carter, Hilary Rodham Clinton, and Linus C. Pauling.

Pamela lives in Toronto, Canada, and works globally helping people with their writing projects. More information is available at www.writertypes.com.

Index

Index

www.ingramcontent.com/pod-product-compliance
Lightning Source LLC
Chambersburg PA
CBHW060012300526
45794CB00003B/1178